# The Swinging Sporran

# The Swinging
# Sporran

*A lighthearted guide
to the basic steps
of Scottish reels
and country dances*

## RODDY MARTINE AND
## ANDREW CAMPBELL

BIRLINN

This edition published in 2006 by
Birlinn Limited
West Newington House
10 Newington Road
Edinburgh
EH9 1QS

Reprinted 2007

www.birlinn.co.uk

First published in 1973 by Wolfe Publishing Limited, London

ISBN13: 978 1 84158 489 8
ISBN10: 1 84158 489 4

British Library Cataloguing-in-Publication Data
A catalogue record for this book is available from the British Library

Printed and bound in Great Britain by Cox & Wyman Ltd, Reading

# *Contents*

# Introduction

A NATION'S songs and dances are at the very centre of its culture and are said to represent the innermost character of a people. In England, for example, they skip around maypoles in the summer months. In the Middle East they use seven veils (the climate is warmer there). America has its Dixie and Ragtime. In Spain they have Flamenco. In Scotland we dance reels.

It must be emphasized that this booklet is not a serious guide for the Scottish Country Dance Societies. The Reels covered in the following pages are the elementary ones, the sort likely to be encountered at most highland and many lowland gatherings, and the information offered is geared to 'inform' the average party-goer who thinks that a 'poussette' is some sort of Siamese cat.

*A. Campbell & R. Martine*
*Edinburgh 1973*

5

# History

THE ORIGINS of the Scottish Country Dance are vague. Historians claim that the Reel of Four is connected with the religious practices of the Druids, and this theory is further supported by the discovery close to the Standing Stones on Orkney of an ancient emblem illustrating the chain figure. This formation, which is similar to the serpentine chain on the Caduceus rod, is particularly significant since the Standing Stones are associated with astronomy, worship and dance.

*The Chain Figure*

It is further believed that, when the male dancer raises his arms above his head and leaps up and down, he is enacting the movements of an ancient stag—a further link with the Druids for whom the stag was a symbol of manhood. Two men setting to and turning one another in the Reel of Four represent two stags battling for the attentions of a doe.

*Ancient Stag*

6

It may well be therefore that Scottish Country Dancing would be more correctly entitled Druid Country Dancing. Furthermore, it is interesting to speculate that a Foursome Reel may well be the enactment of a primitive religious or fertility rite, and may well represent something totally unspeakable

*Druid Country Dancing*

The Druids are known to have held a number of curious festivals. One of these, held on May Day, involved a boy facing east and throwing a piece of bread covered in custard over his shoulder in a westerly direction and calling out, 'This to thee, O Raven!' What happened to the youth after this has not been recorded. Another strange festival took place in Perthshire when Druids are known to have danced round small conical hills. Until about the eighteenth century the anniversary of these meetings was held on Hallowe'en.

The sword dance, legend tells us, originates from the days of MacBeth, when Malcolm Canmore, a Celtic prince, who had slain one of MacBeth's chiefs at the battle near Dunsinane in 1045, felt so pleased with himself that he crossed his dead enemy's sword with his own and danced around them. He must have been spotted by a passing newspaper reporter because his actions were widely publicized and so impressed the general public that he was almost immediately crowned king in succession to MacBeth.

The Scottish Church strongly disapproved of dancing and all forms of merriment, so that it is difficult to establish what was danced, where, why, or how, before 1700. Anything that remotely resembled a dance was immediately associated with witchcraft and the powers

7

of darkness, and in some cases this was perfectly justified. From the pulpit, the Calvinists denounced all dancing as evil and detrimental to the soul's future potential, and as their political influence grew, the strength of their belief became almost fanatical.

Nevertheless, many Scottish landowners were Catholic or Episcopalian, and over the years paid little attention to the doctrines of the Scottish church. It is known that Longwise dancing was popular in the Court of the Stewart kings, and in 1580, King James VI is on record as having paid £100 to one William Hudson for 'teaching us to dance'. The Court of Mary Queen of Scots, under the frown of John Knox, had introduced a number of dances from France, since many of her followers were of the French Court. Basque dancing has left a permanent impression with the 'Pas de Basque', although there is a patriotic school of thought that the marked similarity between the dances of the Scots and the dances of the Basques indicates that the Scots taught the Basques how to dance.

At the time of Mary Queen of Scots, the 'Ring' dance was a great favourite with farming folk in the south of Scotland. This is the ordinary circle formation encountered in the dances of many countries. Chronicles tell us that it was commonly danced in fields at harvest time to the accompaniment of bagpipes. The similarity of this sort of dance with those of other nations has a great deal to do with the gypsies, tinkers and wandering musicians who carried them from country to country, and the soldiers who brought back variations from their European wars.

In Scotland, highland influences (to some extent created from the necessity to keep warm in the winter months) played a considerable part in developing steps and tunes, and these gradually passed down from the noble families, who had the time to experiment with them, to the lower orders to become the dances of the Scottish people. As such many have survived, but most of the reels we dance today were only widely popularized as social dances at the dawning of the twentieth century, and in some cases even later.

The reels danced through the centuries were varied, and in most cases original to the areas in which they were popular. For example, if a particularly unusual happening took place in a village, a dance was often thought up to record the event. One reference book we encountered lists more than 500 different country dances.

To a great extent these steps and dances were passed down from father to son by word of mouth, and in the last century by dancing masters at village schools. At Scottish gatherings and celebrations reels were danced, and it is sad that to a great extent the popularity of these ceilidghs, kirns and wedding feasts has died out to be replaced by the more formal occasions and 'pop' sessions.

In the last century, most towns had public dances throughout the winter months, perhaps once a fortnight, and these were attended not only by townsfolk, but by the people from the surrounding countryside. In the Scottish Borders, at the completion of a harvest, farming folk would hold a 'kirn' or 'harvest home' to celebrate. These took place in barns and granaries and were times of great merriment.

With the popularity of the Hunt evolved the Hunt Ball, and today, although many of the hunts have died out, the balls are so popular that they are invariably over-subscribed.

Ceilidghs were an essential part of the life in the Highlands and Islands. Everybody was welcome and would come from miles around, and all took part by either singing, playing a musical instrument or dancing. Aside from these, many lairds held an annual ball for their tenants which were to a great extent family gatherings. These dances would start about 9 p.m. and could go on to 6 a.m.

After wedding ceremonies there would always be singing and dancing, and on certain Western Isles a particularly amusing dance would take place. This involved the bride and groom dancing a reel with their guests towards the end of the evening. The bride would suddenly be spirited away by her attendants and her place taken in the set by one of the bridesmaids. The bride would then be put to bed, and as soon as the bridegroom became aware of her disappearance, he would be taken to her by the men. The theory behind this was to cheat the local fairies, a particularly active variety who are notorious for pinching west coast brides on their wedding nights, and contrast dramatically with the species found elsewhere who usually prefer the grooms.

After Highland Games there would be local ceilidghs, and today's annual social gatherings have evolved in many cases from these. Local landowners also held parties for house guests and neighbours, and these ceilidghs developed into such occasions as the Argyllshire Gathering Balls (held before and after the Oban Games; now held on one night only), and the Aboyne Ball (held before Braemar). Similarly, balls were and still are held at Lochaber, Skye, Donside, Inverness (the Northern Meeting), in Perthshire (The Perth Hunt Balls), and at Forfar (The Angus Ball, now the Angus Private Subscription Dance).

In London, the first Caledonian Ball took place in 1849 at the invitation of the 6th Duke and Duchess of Atholl. Originally a small private gathering for the purpose of collecting funds for charity, this has now grown into the largest ball of the London season where Scots gather from all over the world to dance reels.

Aside from these major social events, however, the dancing of reels is no longer the prominent social pastime it once was. This is inevitable with the upsurge of 'pop' and modern dancing, but the important fact remains that reels still hold their own. When the Royal Scottish Country Dance Society was formed in 1926, reels were very much on the decline, and full credit should be given to the Society for their splendid work in preserving and popularizing so many reels and dances which are so much a part of Scotland's heritage. Anybody who has recently attended a Scottish gathering will be fully aware of just how popular and fashionable certain reels have become. They might even become alarmed at what can only be described as the 'tribal' enthusiasm that is displayed, especially among the younger generation.

# *Dress*

MOST SCOTS are related to a clan, and although in some cases the connections are rather dubious, the majority are eligible to wear some sort of tartan. Each clan has its own tartan, and often clan chieftains and their eldest sons have their own personal tartans which serve mainly to confuse people who have been swatting up on tartan spotting.

The kilt, Scotland's national dress, is a familiar sight. Basically, it should hang from the hips at the same level all round, but inevitably it tends to hang down at the front and up at the back, or up at the front and down at the back depending upon the anatomy of the wearer.

*Depending upon the anatomy of the wearer*

Correctly, it should just touch the ground at the front when the wearer kneels, which of course the Scot should only do when proposing or in the presence of Royalty to receive a knighthood.

In 1746, the Act of Proscription which was passed by an English Parliament after the defeat of Prince Charles Edward at Culloden

*Trews*

forbade the wearing of tartan and the kilt, and decreed that grey
trews or knee breeches must be worn instead—from this comes the
story that the 'kicking' movement of the Pas de Basque represents
the Highlander 'kicking off' his humiliating apparel.

This legislation affected all Scots with the exception of those who
had fought on the Government side (such as the soldiers of The
Black Watch). In time, various new regiments were formed and
allowed to adopt an approved tartan. Nevertheless, the clan system
and everything akin to it was suppressed by law, and this indignity
lasted thirty-six years.

When the law was finally abolished, thanks to the perseverance of
the Duke of Montrose, a number of clans had forgotten what their
tartans looked like. Around 1840, however, tartans suddenly became
the height of fashion, and this enthusiasm was heightened by the
visit of King George IV to Edinburgh in 1822 when he appeared at a
levée at Holyrood sporting a colossal kilt worn over pink tights. It
was about this time that John Sobieski Stuart wrote his *Vestiarium
Scoticum* (published later in 1842 by William Tait), and it was he
who furnished many highland families with tartan designs. To this
manuscript can be credited much of the tartan confusion that exists
even to this day.

In order that a tartan should have a weathered and mellowed appearance, a 'new' kilt should be buried for at least six months in a peat bog or similar soil. Such is the texture and weave of genuine tartan cloth that a kilt should be able to survive in all conditions for many generations, and testimony to this can be found in such areas as Culloden where samples of tartan are still unearthed long after their slaughtered owners have disintegrated.* Nowadays, however, it is possible to purchase pre-buried tartan cloth of satisfactory 'muted' tones.

Another aspect of highland dress is the Trews. It is believed that these came into fashion with horse riding, and various regiments have retained them as uniform. Anybody who has ever tried to ride a horse while wearing the kilt should appreciate the innovation.

On the subject of the kilt and trews, one must touch on an age old and joky subject. Tradition has it that the kilt should have no undergarment. Nicety suggests that when dancing reels this should not be so. If tradition is followed, the wearer should take care how

*The wearer should take care how he
allows his kilt to swing*

---

\* *Material should of course be washed after burial—preferably in 'peaty' water which can be found in highland burns and bathrooms, or purchased in cans from American supermarkets.*

*The wearing of trews under the kilt can of course
be carried a little too far*

he sits, and how he allows his kilt to swing. Needless to say, few
Scots pay much attention to this subject and are always amazed at
the interest displayed by the uninformed. In some cases, however,
dancers have taken to wearing a short pair of trews in a matching
tartan.

A variety of evening dress is likely to be seen at highland dances.
In the West Highlands and Argyll, a jabot (a frilly lace thing tied
round the neck) is the approved dress, although in Inverness and the
Northern Highlands, a wing collar and a black bow tie is considered
correct. In Perthshire, a white bow tie and wing collar is allowed for
natives of the county. South of Perthshire, the wearing of the kilt is
considered by many as being incorrect.

A variety of jackets are worn: the Dress Doublet, the Montrose
Doublet, the Argyll Doublet or Prince Charles Coatee. A number of
individuals have their own unusual variations on these, so one should
never register surprise at some of the apparitions one is likely to
encounter.

As most ladies will agree, pockets do not look particularly stylish
on a dress. Thus handbags and purses came about, and in a similar
way, sporrans evolved. There are a variety of these, and an interesting
pastime for wallflowers is sporran spotting—a great deal about the
character of the wearer can be discerned from his choice of sporran.

*Dress Doublet with Jabot    Prince Charles Coatee    Highland Inherited*

*Sealskin Swinger        Pigskin Passionate        Otterhead Special*

*Highland Horse                    Lone Ranger*

In passing, one must mention the Sgiandubh (pronounced 'Skeendoo'). This is a small dagger which is worn in the sock or 'hose' as a decorative inconvenience. It is usually decorated in silver and cairngorms. When the blade is drawn from its scabbard, tradition has it that blood should be spilt. This is sometimes very tempting, but not advisable, and it is better to keep the blade undrawn. Highland rebels and soldiers are known to have disregarded this custom and employed the sgiandubh along with a fork for eating purposes. Generally, however, the sgiandubh tends to be rather a nuisance when reeling since it invariably slips down to the bottom of the sock when the wearer is being particularly energetic.

Dress for ladies tends to be dictated by the fashion of the day. Society influences dictate that for evening wear a long dress with full skirt, gloves and sash are correct. When a girl is 'coming out' she should wear white. She will then progress rapidly towards wearing black. Nobody, however, should ever dictate individual fashion to a lady, and we therefore consider that it should be left to personal taste. It is interesting, however, to note that a number of highland ladies have had tartan dresses made.

The question of the shoulder over which a lady should wear her sash is a controversial subject. Generally speaking, it is safer for her to wear her sash over the left shoulder, but if she is the eldest daughter of a major family, an army officer's wife, or some similar exceptional case, she can wear it over her right shoulder. On no account should she tie it round her waist. Men, in a similar vein, should resist the urge to wear a plaid at dances as these are worn only by military bandsmen nowadays. In the last century they were commonly worn on smart occasions, but in those days at many dances there would be a break half way through the evening for the dancers to change into fresh clothes. Dancing reels is a very energetic and hot activity!

# *Preparation*

TO START with, an ambitious reel dancer must learn to look and act correctly. In the following pages the basic steps and dances will be explained, but to begin with, a professional appearance must be achieved.

*Incorrect*          *Incorrect*          *Correct*

The correct stance for the male is illustrated. The female should not adopt this stance as it is not particularly feminine. Instead, an expression of wide-eyed bewilderment should be adopted. Somebody once wrote that dancing was making love to music. Although in polite circles (but there are not many of these nowadays) reeling might be considered as a refined art, it is more commonly a means of social flirtation and open warfare between the sexes. A female will be thrown about amid swinging sporrans and hairy knees, and should she break a leg as she hurtles through an open window, she will be

17

expected to pick herself up and carry on dancing. Thus the Scottish maid has hardened herself over the years to meet the treatment, and has learnt to encounter her partner on the dance floor with a mixture of cunning and concealed strength.

Female reelers can be split into three categories: (A) Braw Scots lassies, (B) Wee Scots lassies, and (C) Debutantes. From the male point of view the former are to be preferred as they provide a soft landing. (B) tend to be little and lethal, and (C) is always happier in the rhododendrons.

*Braw Scots lassie*     *Wee Scots lassie*     *Debutante*

Where movements are concerned, a lady should give the impression that she is 'moving round on wheels'. It is considered unladylike to 'bounce'.

It is very important for the male to make the right kind of noise. This takes the form of a blood curdling shriek. Try pursing your lips and shouting 'SOUP' very loudly in a contralto voice. Substitute a 'Y' for the 'S', and you should achieve just about the right sound. These noises are very important as they inform the surrounding

*Moving round on wheels*

countryside that one is enjoying oneself. No matter how enthusiastic they are, however, ladies should not indulge in these noises.

Another popular cry is 'Oi, Oi, Oi!' uttered by the male when setting to another male (also on occasions when setting to his partner). There is no credible translation for this sound, but it is thought to have something to do with the seals off Oban.

# The Country Dances

WE HAVE NOW come to the explanatory section of this book, consisting of a detailed introduction and an explanation of four reels and twelve country dances. The difference between a reel and a country dance is that a reel is a ring dance and a country dance is a long dance or 'set' dance. The reels are named after the number of dancers in the square while the country dances are named after the tunes to which they were originally performed.

For the complete beginner to learn to dance entirely from this book is expecting too much. This section is more aimed at the person who has done one or two dances under pressure and who always feels completely lost. Those who have not been this unfortunate, but suspect that they may be in the near future, can protect themselves from becoming ruffled and will be able to hold down the rising panic by diligent use of the following pages.

# *The Set*

IN SCOTTISH Country Dancing the men and women form two lines facing each other, with the band at the top. The men are usually on the left as one faces the band. Each man stands opposite his partner and the couples are numbered off from the top into 'sets', usually of six couples each. The dance is then performed by each 'set' separately, with the top couples of every 'set' all starting off the dance at the same time.

A country dance comprises a 'routine' carried out by the top couple of each 'set' with the two couples next below them—the remaining being separate. If one considers the couple enacting the 'routine' as the 'star' performers, and the other two couples as supporting actors, then you have an idea of their relative importance. One important requirement of the 'routine' is that the couple performing must start above the couples they intend to dance with and end up between them.

Band

Men        Women

①             ①      Top

②             ②

③             ③

④             ④

⑤             ⑤

⑥             ⑥   Bottom

When the man and the woman of the first couple have completed this routine, they finish up standing respectively between the men and the women of couples 2 and 3. They then immediately repeat the routine with the next two couples, 3 and 4, similarly ending up between them, and so on—until they reach the end of their 'set', and stand at the bottom of it.

Meanwhile, couple No. 2 (now at the top) wait until they see that the first couple has finished dancing with couples 3 and 4. They then start off the routine with couples 3 and 4, progressing down the 'set' in the same way until they in turn reach the bottom of it. Each couple follows in turn, until the original top couple finds itself back at the top of the 'set' again. The band leader usually watches the nearest 'set', and plays until he sees that each couple has had a turn at the top.

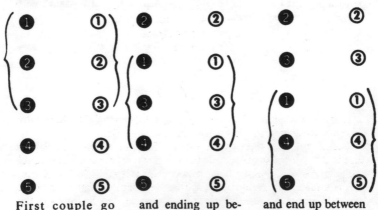

First couple go through 'routine' using couples 2 and 3 . . .

and ending up between them. Repeat using couples 3 and 4 . . .

and end up between them. Thus they continue.

22

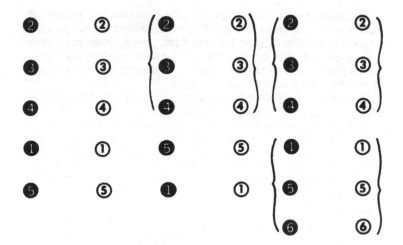

| When couple 1 are between 4 and 5 . . . | couple 2 can now start using couples 3 and 4. Couple 1 move to the bottom if there are only five couples in the set . . . | or carry on using couples 5 and 6. |

At this point the reel has been completed. Normally, however, the band is encouraged to play it through again.

Scottish Country Dances are social affairs, in which each person dances with all the other members of the 'set' on a completely equal basis. Strangers at the beginning of a reel are often friends by the end, and, of course, friends at the beginning are often enemies by the end. It is this aspect of Scottish Country Dancing that has caused the amazing revival we have seen since the beginning of the century.

In Scottish Social Dancing, the action—i.e. where to go, what to do, and when to do it—is more important than the style and steps. For example, in some dances the man must lead the woman down between the lines of the set and up again. It is more important that the man should know when, and in which reels he should do this rather than to know that when leading the woman he should hold her right hand in his right hand.

Consequently, what follows is to a great extent 'non-technical', and is not recommended to the perfectionist in a Scottish Country Dance Society. Explanations are aimed at the complete beginner and the semi-skilled performer who wishes to get the maximum enjoyment and minimum embarrassment out of dancing reels with others of varying skill and enthusiasm. Although an introductory piece on the basic movements is provided it is suggested that the beginner now turns to the Dance section (page 49) and studies a few of the routines in order to get some idea of the action before he studies the style.

# Introduction and Method

THE COUNTRY DANCE routine is just like any other dance routine in that the object is to make it as smooth as possible. The steps and movements outlined in this section are to assist the dancer in making his or her routine flow more smoothly. The method should be secondary. Therefore, if the dancer finds it easier to use a personal style or step to keep the reel flowing, so much the better.

Bear in mind, however, that as in any 'sport', unless you play the strokes or shots the correct way, you will never pass a certain degree of sophistication. Scottish Dancing is very energetic, and one has to be nimble on one's feet. It is, therefore, essential to have a comfortable pair of shoes to dance in. Feet have been known to swell up after a first enthusiastic attempt, and stockinged feet are recommended for practising. Below are some basic steps and movements used in most of the country dances to follow.

## The Pas de Basque

The verb 'to set' (to someone) must not be confused in Scottish Country Dancing with the noun 'a set' as explained earlier. To 'set'

means to stand opposite the person to whom one is dancing and to complete two Pas de Basque steps. To 'set and turn' is a very common move in the dances and requires the performer to set to someone, and then to turn them with two hands. Incidentally, it is not only courteous to set to someone who is setting to you but it is an important part of the dance.

**Set**

*(Symbol represents a couple setting to one another)*

***and turn***

*(Symbol represents the couple turning clockwise)*

First of all it is necessary for the dancer to have some idea of the Pas de Basque. There follows an involved description of how to build up the movements until one achieves the complete step. The description is supported by foot diagrams, and it should be noted that the 'black' foot is the one which supports the weight. The Pas de Basque is a difficult step, and trouble should be taken to master it. Failing this, however, a step must be developed which moves in time to the music.

The Pas de Basque is danced on one spot with movements to either side. Stand heels together, feet slightly turned out. To help balance, while practising, hands can be placed on the hips though this is not encouraged when actually dancing in a set. The music for the step is 'and one, two three' being one bar of a reel. A diagram is given below for each beat.

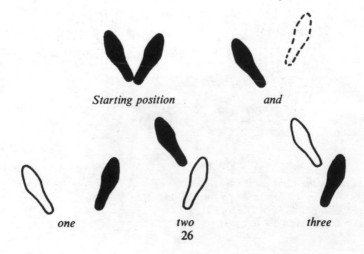

*Starting position*  *and*

*one*  *two*  *three*

**'and'**
*Left foot remains as in the starting position while the right foot is lifted off the ground and held out at about 2.00.*

**'one'**
*The right foot is now placed on the ground about 1 ft. from the left foot and the weight is transferred to the right foot. The left foot remains where it is.*

**'two'**
*The left foot is now placed at an angle to the right foot with the heel of the left foot next to the toes of the right foot. The weight is transferred to the left foot.*

**'three'**
*The feet are not moved, but the weight is transferred back on to the right foot.*

27

The whole exercise is now repeated in reverse. The left foot is put in the 'and' position, and a step of about twelve inches taken to the left. The movement ends up as shown in the diagram below with the weight on the left foot, ready to start again. The step, as you will have realized by now is relatively complicated because of its unusual rhythm. However, as explained so far it is rather lifeless and flat footed. Thus, to those who think that they have mastered this beginners movement it is suggested that they try it on their toes as shown below. (*Read from top left round the arrow to bottom left.*)

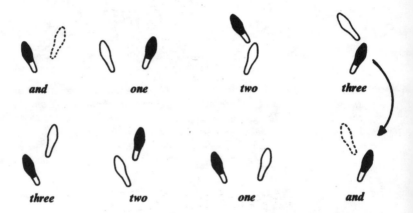

Furthermore, the left foot when brought into the angled position of '*two*' can be placed much closer to the right foot so that the heel of the left foot is above the toes of the right foot. Similarly, the right foot can be placed in reverse so that the right heel is above the left toes.

To get still more life into the movement so that the body is going slightly up and down in time with the beat of the music straighten the left leg on '*and*', bend the right leg on '*one*', straighten left leg on '*two*', bend right leg on '*three*', straighten right leg on '*and*', bend left leg on '*one*', straighten right leg on '*two*' and bend left leg on '*three*', etc.

The final movement is a delicate rhythmical step with the '*and*' more of a kick outwards before taking a step sideways.

The Pas de Basque, as explained, is a step done on the spot. It is therefore necessary to develop a step for travelling from one place to another. This is called 'The Travel Step'. It must be said at this stage that it is possible to do the Pas de Basque while moving

28

forward, backward and round and round on the spot. These movements may come naturally, but it is worth attempting to master the forward movement as the backward movement can always be achieved by turning round and going in the other direction.

*It is, of course, easy to be over enthused*

# The travel step

THREE

TWO

This step has the same rhythm as the Pas de Basque ('*and one, two three*') and is fairly similar to it. The following diagram must be read by starting at the bottom. Each movement is explained as follows.

## ONE

Step forwards is taken with right foot. The weight is on the right foot and the toe of the left foot.

ONE

## TWO

Left foot is brought forward up almost behind the right foot, weight as in 'one'.

AND

## THREE

Weight transferred momentarily to left toe while a small step is taken with the right foot. Then weight is put back on the right foot and left toe.

## AND

Rise on to right toe and swing left foot ready to take a step forward with left foot.

THREE

As in the diagram the step then continues leading with the left foot.

TWO

This is a highly popular step even though it would be frowned upon by Country Dance Societies. It is recommended in one other book* where it is called the Travelling Pas de Basque. J. F. and T. M. Flett say 'This step was used frequently in Country Dances and Reels in all parts of the country, and is still used at the Highland Balls. It was never taught by dancing teachers, and was, indeed, generally regarded by them as "bad dancing", but it is in fact a very safe and suitable step for use on a highly polished floor.'

ONE

---

\* *J. F. and T. M. Flett*, Traditional Dancing in Scotland (*Routledge & Kegan Paul, London*).

# Turning and swinging and the grips

## The turn

The woman puts her hands straight out face down and the man takes hold of her hands from underneath with his thumbs pointing towards her. Both then do a complete revolution using the travel step in a clockwise direction.

## The Swing

For the swing there are six different types of grip which will be listed. The swing itself requires you to hold your partner in one of the following grips and to revolve (or swing round) once, twice, three or more times using *the travel step*. A well executed swing in any of the forms below is one of the most enjoyable parts of a Scottish Country Dance. The little symbol with each explanation is the one we will use to represent that grip when explaining the dances.

### 1. Crossed wrists grip

The man crosses his wrists with his thumbs pointing upwards. The woman takes hold of his hands thumbs up, so that her right hand is in his right hand. The arms should be bent and the elbows held quite close to the body as the couple swing clockwise.

### 2. Crossed forearms grip

The man cups his right hand underneath and behind the woman's right elbow. The woman does the same to the man, so that their right forearms are in contact. The two left hands then grip one another, thumbs up, over the top of the crossed forearms.

*N.B.:* This grip is equivalent to No. 1 and can be used in nearly all the same situations. It is considered a superior grip and its use should be increased. However, it is important to note that the man's right thumb is not used in this grip. There is a tendency for the man to place his right thumb on the woman's biceps and grip her upper arm. This should be *absolutely* forbidden as it causes large bruises to appear the following day.

### 3. *Arms linked*

(*A*) *Right arms linked*

The couple link right arms at the elbow and swing clockwise. The woman is allowed extra support in times of stress by holding her right wrist with her left hand.

*or*

The couple link left arms at the elbow and swing anti-clockwise.

*(B) Right forearms linked*

The couple cup their partners' right elbows in their right hands so that their forearms are in contact (as in 2).

*or*

The couple cup their partners' left elbows in their respective left hands so that their forearms are in contact.

*N.B.:* Remember that the man is not allowed to use his right or left thumb in this grip.

### 4. *Reverse arms grip*

Both partners place their left arms behind their backs and then link right arms. The right hands are then placed in the opposite left hands behind the partner's back. Couples swing clockwise.

### 5. *Policeman's halt grip*

Both partners raise their right arms as in a policeman's halt sign. Partners then join right hands and swing so that forearms are almost vertical.

It must be remembered that any grip variation is allowed and often applauded as long as the partners remain on their feet before, during and after the swing! For example, the McColl Grip (or woman with broken right arm grip) requires the man to place his right arm around the woman's waist, holding her right shoulder in his left hand. She may place her left hand on his right shoulder if she needs more support.

# Terminology

In the rest of the book we will be continually referring to the man and the woman in the 1st couple who are doing the routine. We have therefore developed a simplifying terminology. The couple doing the routine are (M) and (F) and are equivalent to (1) and (1) respectively. We will call (M) the 'Male' and (F) the 'Female'. All the other dancers will be referred to by their full description, i.e., (3) is man No. 3 and (2) is woman No. 2.

# Corners

As we have already explained most country dance routines are enacted in sets of five or six by one couple with two other couples. The two supporting couples form the corners of a square in which the routine is performed. For this reason dancers are often named after their corner rather than their number in the set. In the diagram Ⓜ and Ⓕ are about to do a routine with couples 2 and 3.

In this case the 2nd man (②) and the 3rd woman (③) become first corners and the 3rd man (③) and 2nd woman (②) become the second corners. Just to confuse you at this point the first of the two supporting couples in this case (② and ②) are sometimes called the top couple and the second of the supporting couples can be called the bottom couple. However, this terminology is very confusing and misleading, so perhaps we had better ignore it.

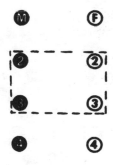

### *Swing corners*

Female swings 1st corner (man No. 2), male swings 1st corner (woman No. 3), both swing right arms linked.
*or*
  Couple swing 1st corners, right arms linked.

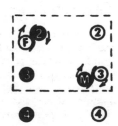

37

Couple swing in the middle, left arms linked.

*or*

Couple swing each other, left arms linked.

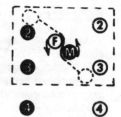

Female swings 2nd corner (male No. 3), male swings 2nd corner (woman No. 2), both swing right arms linked.

*or*

Couple swing 2nd corners, right arms linked.

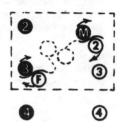

### *Set and turn corners*

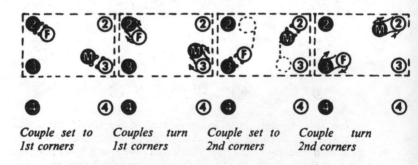

*Couple set to 1st corners*  *Couples turn 1st corners*  *Couple set to 2nd corners*  *Couple turn 2nd corners*

From the above the reader should be able to grasp the basic idea of a square and the limited area in which the routine is undertaken. The 4th couple has been shown in each diagram to give the impression of a set of couples lined out down the page and to show that the routine only involves three couples, the fourth couple down taking no part at all.

# The Figure of Eight

### The Figure of Eight with Three

In technical terms this is called a reel of three, but is in fact commonly known simply as a figure of eight. It is danced either with two men and one woman, or two women and one man.

(A) Two men and one woman

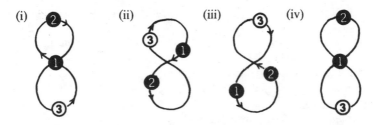

(B) Two women and one man

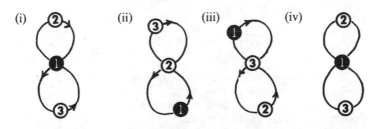

The dancers start in position (i) and move round the figure following their arrows. They reach position (ii) then (iii). When they have each been round the figure once and have reached position (iv), which is the same as (i) and therefore their starting points, they have completed one figure of eight.

### The Figure of Eight with Four

Likewise this is properly called the reel of four and is a double figure of eight, traced out by two couples. The dancers pass right shoulders with a member of the opposite sex and left shoulders with the same sex.

In a similar fashion as before the dancers start in position (i) and

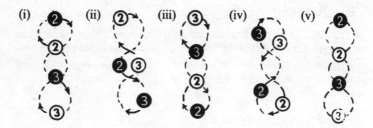

(i) (ii) (iii) (iv) (v)

follow their arrows, each tracing out the dotted 'figure of four'. They pass through positions (ii), (iii) and (iv), and when they have returned to their original positions, as in (v), they have finished.

### Half Figure of Eight with Four

One can easily see that when the dancers have reached position (iii) they are half way through their figure of eight with four. In some country dances this movement is used so that two people may change places. In this case man No. 2 and woman No. 3 have changed.

### Weaving Figure of Eight

The figure-of-eight movement can also be done with one person weaving in and out of two stationary people. The two stationary dancers are usually of the same sex.

# The Circle

The circle is a very straightforward formation. Three couples join hands and dance four Pas de Basque to their left and then four Pas de Basque back again.

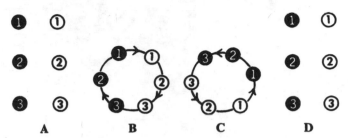

A    B    C    D

The circle should always move off to the left—to move to the right first is to invoke witchcraft (*widdershins*).

# Casting off

This is a movement where the couple go round the outside of the lines of the set in order to move down either one or two places. The male must turn to his left and progress down the outside of the set, while the female must turn to her right before moving down the outside.

An equivalent, but opposite movement is that of 'casting up'. Here the couple turn towards the bottom of the set and then travel up the set as many places as are specified, i.e., normally one or two.

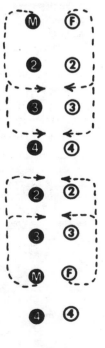

41

# Teapots and the wheel

Teapots is the name given to a particular movement used in the Duke and Duchess of Edinburgh (so called because of the correct posture which should be taken up by the dancer to resemble a teapot. The left or right hand should be placed on the hip so that the arm represents a handle, and the other arm should be elevated to form a spout. The left hand is rarely placed on the hip when dancing nowadays). The popularity of this dance has meant that the name 'teapots' is used for a similar movement in some other reels, namely the wheel (Teapot of four).

A teapot is a movement where three dancers, two of one sex and one of the other, raise and join either their right hands or their left hands in a type of policeman's halt grip, and turn once round using the travel step.

*Right hand teapot of three*

*Left hand teapot of three*

42

Similarly one can have a right-handed teapot of four, and a left-handed teapot of four.

*Right-handed teapot of four*

*Left-handed teapot of four*

# Balancing in line

It is important here to make a distinction between, say, two couples balancing in line and two couples joining hands in line.

In the latter all four dancers are facing the same way and simply join hands so that right hands are held in left hands, and left hands in right hands.

*Joining hands in line*

Balancing in line requires the dancers to face in alternate directions so that they can use the policeman's halt grip, right hands held with right hands, and left hands held with left hands.

*Balancing in line*

# Square chain

This movement takes the form of a square traced out by two couples. They give first their right hands and then their left hands to the dancers they pass. The symbol opposite is the one we will use to represent this movement.

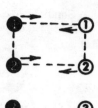

Both couples give right hands to their partners and pass . . .

then they give left hands to their own sex and pass . . .

then right hands to partners and pass . . .

left hands to their own sex and pass . . .

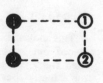

ending up in their original positions.

44

It is worth noting that one has to turn in an unexpected direction in order to keep going round the square. Although it may look simple on paper, one is advised to practise it before a dance.

## Poussette

This is a movement whereby two couples can change places. Both couples take their partners' outstretched hands as in the 'turn'. They Pas de Basque round in a movement akin to a waltz so that they pass each other. The top couple moves down the set, and the bottom couple moves up.

This takes eight bars and when they have completely passed each other, each partner returns to his or her side of the set.

## The Strathspey Steps

For the first half of the foursome, the Glasgow Highlanders, and some of the more obscure country dances, the music is in Strathspey time which has a slower rhythm than reel music. Therefore it is necessary to produce a 'setting step' and a travelling step which is more suited to this rhythm.

### Strathspey Setting Step

There are more than ten different common Strathspey setting steps, but here only one is given.

Hop on your left foot and in time to this rhythm move your right foot—to the side, behind the left calf, in front of the left foot, in front of the left shin, to the side, behind the left calf, in front of the left shin, behind the left calf.

45

Then hop on your right foot and do exactly the same movements with your left foot.

### Strathspey Travelling Step

This is very similar to the Reel Time travelling step done to slower time, but a hop is inserted during the 'and'. The step is therefore *step, close, step, hop—step, close, step, hop*.

The 'step' implying a step forward and the 'close' implying closing the gap between the feet by bringing the back foot almost level with the front foot.

# How to use the Diagrams

THE MAIN difference between the following explanations and any normal Scottish Country Dance book is the use of comprehensive diagrams. In each of the country dances given here a diagram is given for every movement made by the dancers. It is possible to pick out any dancer (it could be ⒡ or ② or ③) and follow his or her movements throughout the dance by going from one diagram to the next.

The dotted lines show how the dancers have just moved to the position they are shown in. Solid lines show the movement which the dancer is about to make.

For example, a diagram may be needed to explain 'top couple go down the outside of their side of the set, go round couple 4 and pass up the middle of the set and back to their original positions'.

We give three possible ways of explaining this diagrammatically.

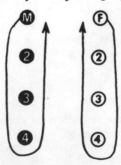

(i)   The diagram shows the dancers as they are just before the movement starts. It explains by a solid line what the dancers do next.

46

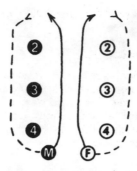

(ii) Here the dancers are shown half way through the movement. The dotted line representing what they have just done. The solid line what they are about to do.

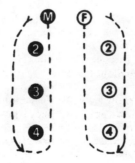

(iii) Finally, the dancers are shown as they would be having completed the movement. The dotted line explaining where they have just moved from.

# Six
# Well-known
# Country
# Dances
# and
# Four
# Reels

# The Duke of Perth

THIS DANCE takes its name from the tune *The Duke of Perth*, the origin of which is not recorded. However, it is also associated with another tune which was popular in the early nineteenth century known as Broun's Reel or the Brownie's Reel to which the dance formations also fit.

Today, the dance is most generally known as The Duke of Perth; but in Angus and East Fife it is often called Broun's Reel, and to the south-west of Lanarkshire, Ayrshire and Galloway it goes under the name of Clean Pea Strae or Pease Strae.

## Basic movements

(A) **Bars** **1–2** Swing partner
         **3–5** Round behind
         **6–8** Left hands
(B)      **9–16** Swing corners
(C)    **17–23** Set and turn corners
(D)    **24–32** Figure of Eight

*(A) Swing partner, round behind, left hands*

Top couple swing crossed wrists or crossed forearms.

*2 BARS*

51

The couple cast off one, male going behind man No. 2, and the female going behind woman No. 2. Couple swing left arms linked, three-quarter turn.

*6 BARS*

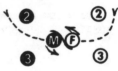

**(B) Swing corners**

The couple then swing first corners right arms linked; male swinging woman No. 3, female swinging man No. 2. Both go once round.

*2 BARS*

 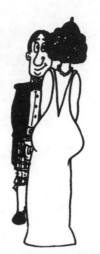 

The couple then swing in the middle; left arms linked, three-quarter turn.

*2 BARS*

The couple then swing 2nd corners; right arms linked, male swinging woman No. 2 and female swinging man No. 3. Both go once round.

*2 BARS*

The couple move out of the swing and face 1st corners.

*2 BARS*

## (C) Set and turn corners

The couple now set to and turn 1st corners; male setting to and turning woman No. 3, and female setting to and turning man No. 2.

*4 BARS*

The couple now set to and turn 2nd corners.

*4 BARS*

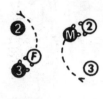

## (D) Figure of Eight

The female does a figure of eight with man No. 2 and man No. 3 while the male does a figure of eight with woman No. 2 and woman No. 3.

*8 BARS*

The female ends up between the two men and the male ends up between the two women. They both then start again repeating the above routine using couples No. 3 and No. 4.

# Reel of the 51st Division

THIS IS A comparatively modern reel, which is becoming increasingly popular at the larger highland dances. It was thought up by two officers of the 51st Highland Division during their internment in a German prisoner-of-war camp (1940–45).

## Basic movements

| | | |
|---|---|---|
| (A) | **Bars 1–2** | Set |
| | 3–5 | Cast off two |
| | 6–8 | Lead up to 1st corner |
| (B) | 9–10 | Set to 1st corner |
| | 11–12 | Turn right hands |
| | 13–14 | Diagonal line across |
| | 15–16 | Swing partner |
| (C) | 17–18 | Set to 2nd corner |
| | 19–20 | Turn right hands |
| | 21–22 | Diagonal line across |
| | 23–24 | Swing partner |
| (D) | 25–32 | Circle |

Ⓜ        Ⓕ

②        ②

③        ③

④        ④

*(A)  Set, cast off two, lead up to first corner*

The couple set, two Pas de Basque, cast off behind their own side and move down below third couple.

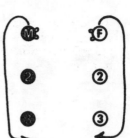

*5 BARS*

The male takes the female's right hand in his right hand and leads her up the set to her 1st corner (man No. 2), then faces his 1st corner (woman No. 3).

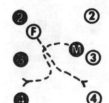

*3 BARS*

*(B)  Set to first corner, turn right hands, diagonal line across, swing partner*

The couple then set to 1st corners and turn them right hands only, using the policeman's halt grip.

*4 BARS*

The couple, having completed their turn and still holding right hands with their corners, join left hands in the middle in a policeman's halt grip. Then all four balance in a diagonal line across the set and dance two Pas de Basque.

*2 BARS*

The couple swing in the middle, crossed wrists, once round. Then face 2nd corners, i.e. male faces woman No. 2 and female faces man No. 3.

*2 BARS*

*(C)* *Set to second corner, turn right hands, diagonal line across, swing partner*

The couple set to 2nd corners and turn them right hands only (policeman's halt grip).

*4 BARS*

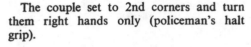

Having completed their turn, the couple then join hands in the middle using policeman's halt grip while still holding right hands with their 2nd corners. The four then balance in a diagonal line across and complete two Pas de Basque.

*2 BARS*

The couple then swing in the middle crossed wrists, once round. The male ends up between the two men, and the female between the two women.

*2 BARS*

57

## (D)  Circle

Couples Nos. 2, 1 and 3 then do a circle—four travel steps to the right and four steps back again.

*8 BARS*

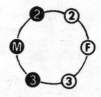

The couple are now in 2nd position and have completed the routine. They start again using couples Nos. 3 and 4.

# The Duke and Duchess of Edinburgh

## Basic movements

(A) **Bars 1–4** Forward—back
          **5** Clap, clap, clap
      **6–8** Swing partner

(B)     **9–16** Figure of eight

(C)   **17–20** Right-hand teapots
     **21–24** Left-hand teapots

(D)   **25–32** Swing corners

(E)   **33–40** Circle

Ⓜ      Ⓕ

❷      ②

❸      ③

❹      ④

### (A) Forward—back, clap, clap, clap, swing partner

Men Nos. 1, 2 and 3 join hands in a line up and down the set, and women Nos. 1, 2 and 3 do likewise. The two lines then move towards each other and back again using four Pas de Basque steps and clapping their hands on the last three beats.

*4 BARS*

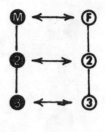

The couple then swing twice round, crossed wrists or crossed forearms. Couples Nos. 2 and 3 also swing twice round.

*4 BARS*

### (B) Figure of Eight

Couples Nos. 2 and 3 *stand still* in their original positions while the male does a figure of eight using men Nos. 2 and 3, starting off by going behind man No. 2, and ending up between them facing down the set. The female enacts the same movement though more slowly, and ends up between women Nos. 2 and 3 facing up the set.

*8 BARS*

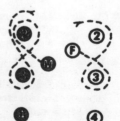

60

## (C)  Right-hand teapots, left-hand teapots

Couple No. 2 and the female do a teapot, *right hands*, once round, while the male and couple No. 3 do a teapot, *right hands*, once round.

*4 BARS*

Male and female now change places and the male does a teapot, *left hands*, with couple No. 2, while the female does a teapot, *left hands*, once round with couple No. 3.

*4 BARS*

## (D)  Swing corners

The couple then swing first corners, right arms linked; male swinging woman No. 3, female swinging man No. 2. Both go round once.

*4 BARS*

(It is important to note that when swinging 1st corners the movement should appear 'smooth and well-oiled'. The couple should come out of their respective teapots so that they pass each other's right shoulder in the middle of the set, and head off towards their respective corners at the same time.)

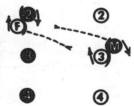

61

The couple then swing in the middle, left arms linked, three-quarter turn.

*2 BARS*

The couple then swing 2nd corners, right arms linked, male swinging woman No. 2 and the female swinging man No. 3. Both go once round.

Female moves across the set and stands between women Nos. 2 and 3, while male moves across and stands between men Nos. 2 and 3.

*2 BARS*

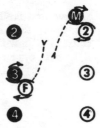

**(E) Circle**

Couples Nos. 2, 1 and 3 then join hands and go four travel steps to the right and four back again.

*8 BARS*

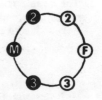

The couple are now placed below couple No. 2 and are ready to start the routine again with couples Nos. 3 and 4.

# *Hamilton House*

THIS IS A flirtatious dance, reputedly started by a young aristocratic lady flirting with her lover and then turning her husband.

## Basic movements

(A) **Bars** 1–2 Female sets to man No. 2
             3–4 Turns man No. 3
             5–6 Male sets to woman No. 2
             7–8 Turns woman No. 3

(B)     9–10 Join hands across
        11–12 Forward—back
        13–16 Swing partner

(C)    17–18 Join hands up and down
        19–20 Forward—back
        21–24 Swing partner

(D)    25–32 Circle

Ⓜ        Ⓕ

❷        ②

❸        ③

❹        ④

63

### (A) Female sets to man No. 2 and turns man No. 3

The female starts the reel. She moves across the set and sets to man No. 2, and then she turns man No. 3.

The male (her partner) remains standing in his place.

*4 BARS*

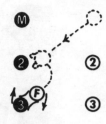

### Male sets to woman No. 2 and turns woman No. 3

The male then copies his partner's movements exactly. He set to woman No. 2 and then turns woman No. 3. Meanwhile, the female, having completed her turn, moves round behind man No. 2 to the top of the set.

*4 BARS*

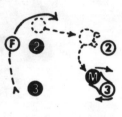

### (B) Join hands across, forward—back, swing partner

As the male completes his turn with woman No. 3, he lets go with his left hand only and joins hands with man No. 3. The three of them form a line across the set facing the top. The female, similarly, moves between the couple No. 2, and joins hands with them, forming a line across and facing down the set.

Both lines then move towards each other and back, using the Pas de Basque.

*4 BARS*

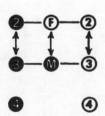

The couple then swing, crossed wrists, one and three-quarters times round; the male placing the female between the two men (Nos. 2 and 3) and himself between the two women (Nos. 2 and 3).

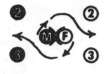

*4 BARS*

### (C) Join hands up and down, forward—back, swing partner

The male joins hands with women Nos. 2 and 3, and the female with men Nos. 2 and 3. They form two lines either side of the set facing each other. Both lines then move forward towards each other and back, using four Pas de Basque steps.

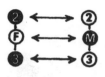

*4 BARS*

The couple then swing, crossed wrists, one and a half times round; the male placing the female between the two women (Nos. 2 and 3) and himself between the two men (Nos. 2 and 3).

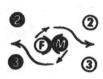

*4 BARS*

### (D) Circle

Finally, couples Nos. 2, 1 and 3 join hands in a circle and go four travel steps round to the left (clockwise) and four travel steps back again.

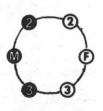

*8 BARS*

The couple are now placed below couple No. 2 and are ready to start the routine again using couples Nos. 3 and 4.

## *Inverness Country Dance*
### also known as *Speed the Plough*

## Basic movements

| | | | | |
|---|---|---|---|---|
| (A) | **Bars 1–4** | Right-hand teapot of four | Ⓜ | Ⓕ |
| | **5–8** | Left-hand teapot of four | | |
| (B) | **9–16** | Down the middle and back | ② | ② |
| (C) | **17–18** | Set to first corners | | |
| | **19–20** | Swing first corners | | |
| | **21–22** | Set to second corners | ③ | ③ |
| | **23–24** | Swing second corners | | |
| (D) | **25–28** | Set in the middle | | |
| | **29–32** | Swing partner | ④ | ④ |

66

## (A)  Right-hand and then left-hand teapots of four

Couples Nos. 1 and 2 do a right-handed teapot of four, once round, four travel steps.

*4 BARS*

Couples Nos. 1 and 2 then change hands and do a left-handed teapot of four once round, four travel steps.

*4 BARS*

## (B)  Down the middle and back

The male takes the female's right hand in his right hand and leads her down the middle between the two lines of the set (four travel steps). The couple then turn inwards and, still holding hands, the male leads the female back up to the top of the set and presents her to her first corner (man No. 2), while himself facing his first corner (woman No. 3).

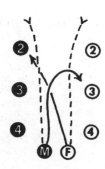

*8 BARS*

## (C) *Set to first corners and swing*

Female sets to first corner (man No. 2), while male sets to his first corner. Both do two Pas de Basque.

*2 BARS*

Couple now swing first corners, crossed wrists or crossed forearms, once round.

*2 BARS*

## *Set to second corners and swing*

The movement is repeated exactly for second corners, the female setting to and swinging man No. 3, and the male setting to and swinging woman No. 2.

*4 BARS*

## (D) *Set in middle, swing partner*

The female then stands between couple No. 2 and the male between couple No. 3, and they set facing each other (four Pas de Basque).

*4 BARS*

68

The couple then swing crossed wrists or crossed forearms in the centre twice round, and the male places the female between women Nos. 2 and 3, and himself between men Nos. 2 and 3.

*4 BARS*

The couple are now below couple No. 2 and are ready to restart the routine with Couples Nos. 3 and 4.

# *Machine Without Horses*

THIS DANCE was recorded in 1772. It is still popular at the Skye Balls and The Northern Meeting.

## Basic movements

(A) **Bars 1–2** Set
       **3–4** Cast off one
       **5–8** Right-hand teapot of four

(B)    **9–10** Set
     **11–12** Cast up one
     **13–16** Left-hand teapot of four

(C)   **17–18** Down the middle
     **19–20** Cast round No. 3
     **21–24** No. 2 follow
              Nos. 1 and 2 change positions

(D)   **25–32** Square chain

70

### (A) Set, cast off one, right-hand teapot of four

The couple set, two Pas de Basque, staying on their own sides of the set. They then cast off behind couple No. 2 and move down one place.

*4 BARS*

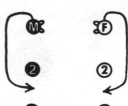

Couples Nos. 1 and 3 do a right-hand teapot of four, once round, using four travel steps.

*4 BARS*

### (B) Set, cast up one, left-hand teapot of four

The couple set, two Pas de Basque, remaining on their own sides of the set. They then cast up behind couple No. 2 to the top of the set.

*4 BARS*

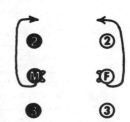

Couples Nos. 2 and 1 then do a left-hand teapot of four, once round, using four travel steps.

*4 BARS*

### (C) *Lead down the middle, cast round No. 3, No. 2 follow and change places*

The male takes the female's right hand and leads her down between the lines of the set. The couple No. 2 follow in the same manner. The male then lets go of his partner's hand and casts round man No. 3. The female similarly casts round woman No. 3.

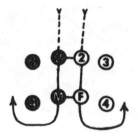

*4 BARS*

The female moves to the front of her original position and casting round the imaginary top of the set, moves into position No. 2. Woman No. 2 follows her, but ends up in position No. 1. The male does likewise on his side with man No. 2 following so that they end up in positions Nos. 2 and 1 resecptively.

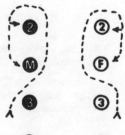

*4 BARS*

72

## (D) Square chain

Couples Nos. 1 and 2 take their partners' right hands and change places. Then the female takes woman No. 2's left hand while the male takes man No. 2's left hand and they change places.

Partners take right hands and change places. Then the men change places and the women change places using left hands. (Refer page 43 for further details.)

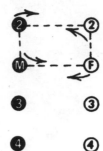

*8 BARS*

Couple No. 1 are now below couple No. 2 and are ready to begin the routine again using couples Nos. 3 and 4.

# The Foursome Reel

## Strathspey movements

(A)  Figure of eight with four
Men face opposite man's partner
Set four Strathspey setting steps

 ①  ①

(B)  Figure of eight with four
Men face their own partners
Set four Strathspey setting steps

(C)  Figure of eight with four
Men face other man's partner
Set four Strathspey setting steps

❷  ②

## Reel movements

(D)  Circle of four twice round

(E)  Set to partner and swing

(F)  Women set and swing

(G)  Set to other person's partner and swing

(H)  Men set and swing

(I)  Set to partners and swing

**(A)**  *Figure of eight with four, men face other man's*
*partner, set*

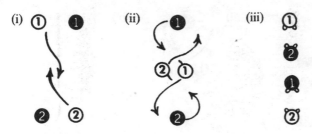

(i)  The women start and pass right shoulders in the centre.

(ii)  The men then follow round in a figure of eight with four. After eight bars, the women have returned to their original positions, and the men stand back to back in the centre facing the other man's partner.

(iii)  Both couples then set four Strathspey steps.

**(B)**  *Figure of eight with four, men face own partners,*
*set*

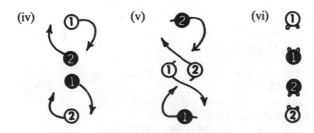

(iv) and (v)  Both couples then complete a figure of eight with four in the orthodox style (i.e., passing right shoulders with the opposite sex and left shoulders with the same sex). After eight bars the women have returned to their original positions and the men remain back to back in the middle facing their partners.

(vi)  Both couples then set four Strathspey setting steps.

## (C)  *Figure of eight with four, men face other man's partner, set*

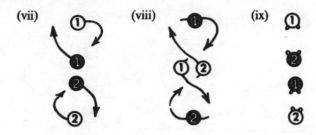

(vii)  (viii)  (ix)

(vii) and (viii) Both couples complete a figure of eight with four in the orthodox style. Women end up in their original places; men back to back in the middle facing each others' partners.

(ix) Both couples then set four Strathspey setting steps.

## (D)  *Circle of four twice round*

The music now changes to a reel tune and both couples join hands in a circle of four and go twice round, the women ending up in their original positions and the men back to back in the middle facing their own partners.

## (E)  *Set to partner and swing*

(i) Both couples then set, eight Pas de Basque.

(ii) Swing reversed arms grip for eight bars.

*Note:* On the last four bars of the Pas de Basque the men will usually raise their hands above their heads and shriek.

During the swing the couple may change hands and go round in the reverse direction after four bars. This breaks the continuity of the swing, but it is often necessary as the swing is liable to gather momentum as it continues.

(i) 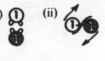  (ii)

76

**(F)   *The women set and swing***

(iii) The two men stand back while the women set eight Pas de Basque.

(iv) The women swing reversed arms grip for eight bars.

(iii)    (iv)

**(G)   *Set to other person's partner and swing***

Woman No. 1 comes out of her swing and faces man No. 2. Similarly woman No. 2 faces man No. 1.

(v) Both couples then set eight Pas de Basque.

(vi) Both couples swing reversed arms grip.

(v)   (vi)

**(H)   *Men set to one another and swing***

(vii)  Now the women stand back while the men set eight Pas de Basque facing each other.

(viii) They then swing clockwise right forearms linked for four bars, and change round to swing anti-clockwise with left forearms linked for four bars.

(vii)    (viii)

**(I)   *Set to partners and swing***

(ix) Finally, men face their own partners and set eight Pas de Basque . . .

(x)  and swing for eight bars reversed arms grip.

(ix)    (x)

# The Eightsome Reel

THIS REEL was arranged by the 6th Duke of Atholl, Lord Dunmore and friends, and based on a former Caledonian reel. It was first popularized at the Royal Caledonian Ball in London in 1890.

## Basic movements

(A) Circle
   Cartwheel
   Set to partner and turn
   Chain

(B) Each woman in the middle for two sessions, in turn

(C) Each man in the middle for two sessions, in turn

(D) Circle
   Cartwheel
   Set to partner and turn
   Chain

The four couples stand in a square and are numbered off 1, 2, 3, 4; No. 1 being the couple standing nearest to the band.

### (A) Circle, cartwheel, set to partner and turn, chain

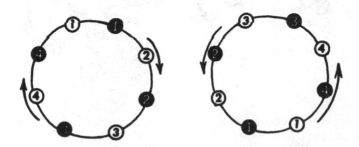

## CIRCLE

The four couples join hands and move four bars round to the left, and then four bars round to the right so that they end up in their original positions.

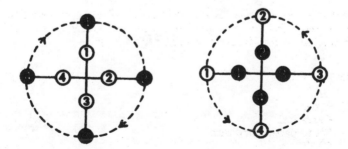

## CARTWHEEL

The man puts his arm round the woman's waist and the women join right hands in the centre, the four couples forming the 'spokes' of a cartwheel. The wheel goes round for four bars (travel step). The women drop their right hands, and the couples swing round to enable the men to join left hands in the middle, still holding their partners round the waist. All four couples move round to their original positions in four bars (travel step).

## SET TO PARTNER AND TURN

Then each couple set facing each other for four bars, and turn (two hands) for four bars (or swing crossed wrists).

## CHAIN

Each couple take right hands and travel round the square giving right and left hands alternately to the people they pass. The men go anti-clockwise, and the women go clockwise. Everyone goes once round and ends up in their original places.

### (B) and (C)   Each woman in the middle for two sessions, in turn, each man in the middle for two sessions, in turn

Now each person goes into the middle alone in turn (women first); the others join hands and circle four Pas de Basque round to the left and four Pas de Basque back again. The person in the middle then sets to and turns (two hands) his or her partner, then sets to and turns the woman or man opposite.

The three persons involved in this last action then do a figure of eight. The same person remains in the middle, and the other dancers circle round again.

When they return to their original positions, the person in the middle sets to and turns the other two men (or women) in the square, and does a figure of eight with them. The next person moves into the middle of the square, the previous person moves out to his or her place, and the same actions are repeated. The first person to go 'in' is woman No. 1, followed by woman No. 2, etc., the last person 'in' will be man No. 4.

## WOMAN NO. 2 IN THE MIDDLE

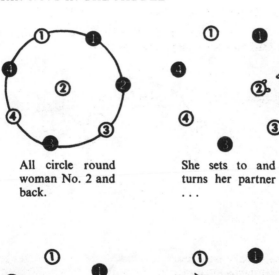

All circle round woman No. 2 and back.

She sets to and turns her partner . . .

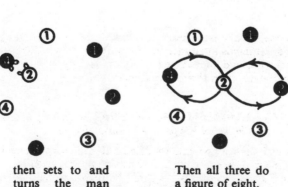

then sets to and turns the man opposite (No. 4).

Then all three do a figure of eight.

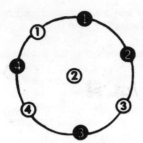

She goes back into the middle and all circle round.

Now she sets to and turns the man next to her partner (man No. 1).

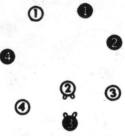

Then sets to and turns the man opposite (man No. 3).

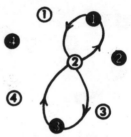

All three do a figure of eight.

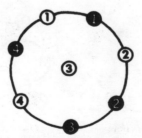

She now goes back to her place and woman No. 3 goes into the middle.

## MAN NO. 4 IN THE MIDDLE

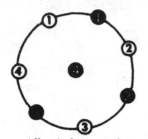

All circle round
man No. 4 and
back again.

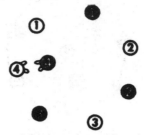

Man sets to and
turns his partner
(woman No. 4)...

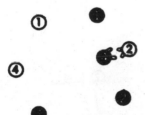

then sets to and
turns the woman
opposite (woman
No. 2).

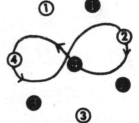

All three do a
figure of eight.

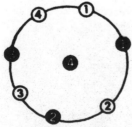

Man No. 4 goes
back in the middle
and all circle
round and back.

Now man sets to
and turns the
woman next to his
partner (woman
No. 1).

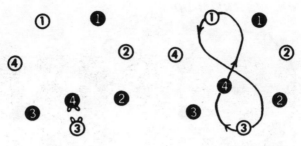

He then sets to
and turns the
woman opposite
(woman No. 3).

All three do a
figure of eight.

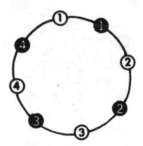

Man then takes
his place in the
circle and all are
ready to dance
(D).

### (D) Circle, cartwheel, set to partner and turn, chain

When the last man (No. 4) has been in the middle, the four couples
repeat the exact movements in (A), ending up with their own partners,
and then swinging reversed arms grip until the music stops.

# The Sixteensome

## Basic movements

(A) Bars 1–8   Circle
           9–16   Double cartwheel
        17–24   Set and turn partner
        25–32   Two chains

(B) Two women in the middle in turn

(C) Two men in the middle in turn

(D) Circle
    Double cartwheel
    Set and turn partner
    Two chains

85

THE SIXTEENSOME, in form, is exactly the same as the eightsome, except that there are twice as many couples. The eight couples stand in a square, two on each side, and are numbered off as shown in the diagram. The side nearest the band is numbered one and two. Each couple is given a number and told 'in' or 'out'.

It is important to remember what your number is all through the reel, and to return exactly to your original position so that the square is re-formed after every movement.

For the purpose of explanation, we are going to number the couples from 1 to 8 so as to be able to distinguish between the couples of the same number. This is *not* how you will be numbered at a dance, so do not be confused.

### (A) *Circle, double cartwheel, set and turn partners, two chains*

All join hands and circle four Pas de Basque round to the left and four back again.

## DOUBLE CARTWHEEL

Then the men put their arms round the women's waists, and women Nos. 1, 3, 5 and 7 join hands to form the axle of a cart-wheel. Couples Nos. 2, 4, 6 and 8 join on to couples Nos. 1, 3, 5 and 7 respectively, as in the diagram. The whole cartwheel goes round once, the 'out' couples on the outside, and the 'in' couples on the inside (8 bars).

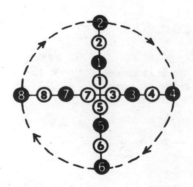

## SET AND TURN PARTNERS

The couples then set—four Pas de Basque—facing each other and turn (two hands), Nos. 2, 4, 6 and 8 on the outside.

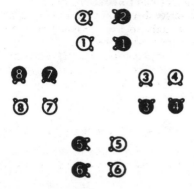

## TWO CHAINS

Two chains are now formed. These are exactly as in the eightsome; couples Nos. 2, 4, 6 and 8 in the outside chain, and couples Nos. 1, 3, 5 and 7 in the inside chain.

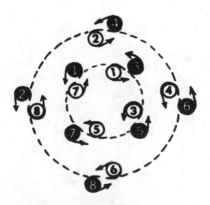

We can note again that the couples who were specified as 'out' are in the outside chain; while the 'in's' form the inside chain.

87

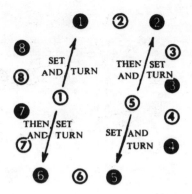

**(B) and (C)** *Two women in the middle in turn, two men in the middle in turn*

Now women Nos. 1 and 5 go into the centre and swing reversed arms grip, while the others join hands and circle round ( four Pas de Basques to the left, and four to the right).

(i)   Both women set and turn their partners, then set to and turn the man opposite.

(ii)   The women (Nos. 1 and 5) now do a figure of eight with their partners and the men opposite their partners (i.e., the men they danced with).

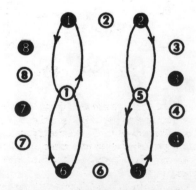

The same women (Nos. 1 and 5) go back in the middle again and swing reversed arms, while the rest join hands and circle round and back (8 bars).

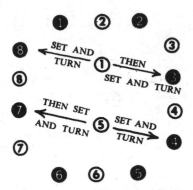

(iii) The women then set to and turn the men next to their partners, and afterwards set to and turn the men opposite. For woman No. 1 this means setting to man No. 8 and man No. 3, while for woman No. 5 this means setting to man No. 4 and man No. 7.

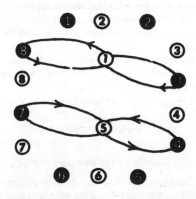

(iv) Setting and turning completed, they do a figure of eight.

This going into the middle, setting, turning, and figure of eight, is enacted by all the dancers in turn, women Nos. 2 and 6 going into the middle next. When all the women have been in the middle—the last pair being women Nos. 8 and 4—the men take their turn, men Nos. 1 and 5 going in first.

When the men are in the middle, they *set to each other four Pas de Basque*, then swing, arms linked for four bars, while the others are circling round (as opposed to the women in the middle who swing reversed arms grip for the whole eight bars).

For the advanced dancers, the odd-numbered men should swing right arms linked the first time they are in, and left arms linked the second time. Similarly, the even-numbered men should swing left arms linked the first time, and right arms linked the second time. The purpose of this is so that the swing should end up with the men facing the women with whom they are to set to first, without having to twist around in an undignified fashion to find their opposite number.

Another point worthy of note is that the men often take this opportunity to attempt to show the women that they are stronger than the man they are swinging with by attempting to hurl him around so fast that he loses control. This nearly always ends up with both men losing control and causing a 'pile up'. A controlled, perfectly balanced swing is always much more effective for wooing the ladies, and violence should only be resorted to if the ladies in general are liable to attribute the better display to the other man. This point is one that applies to all occasions when two or more men are dancing together.

Each dancer, whether male or female, sets to and turns his or her partner, then sets to and turns the person opposite before doing a figure of eight with them. He or she moves back to the middle while the others circle round, and then sets to and turns the person nearest to their partner (on the corner), and the person opposite. Couple No. 3, for example, set to their respective partner and the member of the opposite sex in couple No. 8 the first time, and similarly to couple No. 2 and couple No. 5 the next time.

It is important for each dancer to take note of the people he or she must dance with before the reel begins as the 'square' tends to lose its shape during the reel, and the corners are often difficult to find.

### (D)  Circle, double cartwheel, set and turn partner, two chains

When the last two men (Nos. 4 and 8) have completed their movements in the middle, section (A) is then repeated exactly as explained before.

# EXAMPLES OF MEN NOS. 2 AND 6 IN THE MIDDLE

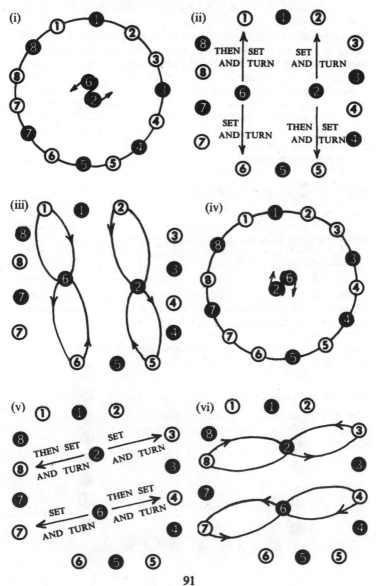

# The Thirtytwosome

THIS REEL is an adaptation of the Eightsome for those dancers who consider themselves sufficiently expert at the Eightsome and Sixteensome. It is sometimes danced at the larger highland balls and at the Caledonian held in Grosvenor House. It does, however, require a considerable amount of space.

As in the sixteensome reel:
(A) Circle
    Cartwheel
    Set and turn partner
    Chain

(B) Four women in the middle in turn

(C) Four men in the middle in turn

(D) Circle
    Cartwheel
    Set and turn partner
    Chain

The dance requires a lot of organization. The formation is again a square, and the basic movements are identical to those of the eightsome and sixteensome.

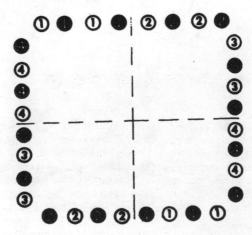

For *the Cartwheel, Setting and Chain,* the sixteen couples divide into four eightsomes. If the square is divided into quarters as in the diagram, then each quarter would form one eightsome.

The square is numbered as shown, which is the same system as for the sixteensome, except that now there are two couples where before there was only one.

As in the sixteensome, all females Nos. 1 step into the centre together for their turn. (All females Nos. 2, 3 and 4 in their respective turns.) As in the sixteensome, they set to their partners and the persons opposite, each one then doing a figure of eight with the two people she has danced with.

The second time they are in the middle it is more difficult. They set to and turn the person who is opposite them within their quarter, and then the person who is opposite on the other side of the square. Following this with a figure of eight.

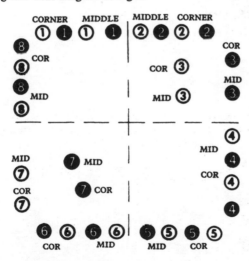

*Taking woman No. 3 in the centre as an example, and renumbering as we did in the sixteensome.* No. 3 (Corner) would set to her partner and the man opposite (No. 8 Corner) the first time. Next time she would set to her opposite number in her quarter (i.e., man No. 2 Corner) and to the man opposite him (man No. 5 Corner). In the meantime, No. 3 Middle would set to and turn first her partner and man No. 8 Middle, and secondly man No. 2 Middle and man No. 5 Middle.

Thus you can see that *Corners only set to and turn Corners, and*

93

*Middles only set to and turn Middles.*

Otherwise, all steps and movements are exactly the same as in the sixteensome. After the last four men have been in the middle for the second time, all circle round to the left (four Pas de Basque) and back again. Couples then divide into their four eightsomes for the final cartwheel, setting, and chain.

It is interesting to note at this stage that on the theory above it is possible to have a sixtyfoursome, 128some, 256some, etc. A sixtyfoursome is danced very occasionally at the larger balls, and a 128some, in which a royal party took part, was once danced at the Northern Meeting when it was held at Aviemore.

If, however, you were to count up the number of people who claim to have danced in it, the reel would seem to have been more like a 150some!

# Six
# Less
# Common
# Reels

THE FOLLOWING six reels are also popular at present in Scotland, but are danced much less frequently than the ones we have already explained. At this stage a good working knowledge of reels is assumed and only the difficult or unusual movements are fully graphically explained.

# The Waltz Country Dance

FIRST KNOWN recording of this dance is in *The Ballroom* published in 1827.

## Basic movements

(A) **Bars 1–16** Set and change, round four
sides of a square

(B)          Join hands in a circle
   **17–18** Hands in and out
   **19–20** Women turn under
   **(17–32** Four repeats)

(C)  **33–40** Waltz round to next couple

This country dance is accompanied by Scottish waltz tunes and has a slightly different step which, basically, is a Pas de Basque to 'one–two–three' instead of to 'and–one–two–three'. Go back to page 26 and try the Pas de Basque leaving out the 'and'. To differentiate, in the following explanation we will call this step the 'de Basque'.

The Waltz Country Dance is a dance similar to the foursome in that it is danced by two couples who start off facing one another.

### (A) *Set and change, round four sides of a square*

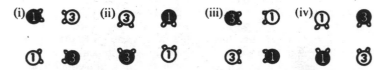

The couples set to each other, two 'de Basque', as in (i), and then change places (two 'de Basque') with the man or woman to whom they were setting. They then set to their partners as in (ii) (two 'de Basque') and change places again, repeating this until they have returned to their original places. (Note that women move anti-clockwise round the square, while men move clockwise.)

When the man and the woman change places as above, the man moves straight forward, and the woman does a waltzing turn anti-clockwise.

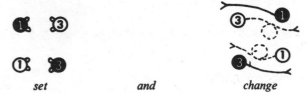

|  set | and | change |

In which case it is important to stand far enough apart so that the women do not collide when turning.

It is, in fact, better if the men can endeavour to move to their places in a curve as shown here.

97

*(B)   Join hands, in and out, women turn under*

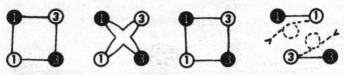

All join hands and balance in a square (i). All then take one step forward with the left foot, swinging their arms into the middle and swaying forward ( 1 bar). The left foot is then brought back again, allowing the arms to swing back (1 bar).

The man takes a step back with his left foot, releasing his left hand, and he turns the woman with his right hand in front of him. She will have stepped forward on her left foot and so will turn clockwise under his right arm (2 bars). Note that this is contrary to the natural waltzing turn, and the woman may find this very difficult to remember. If she leads with her left foot it ought to follow immediately, and she is certain to be long remembered if she gets it right.

All four join hands again and repeat the movement four times. On the fourth time as the woman is spinning merrily under her partner's right hand, he moves into a waltz with her, and they waltz round to face the next couple (8 bars). The whole routine is then repeated.

# *Scottish Reform*
## or *the Prince of Wales*

## Basic movements

| | | | | |
|---|---|---|---|---|
| (A) | **Bars** 1–2<br>3–4 | Turn right hands<br>Balance across | Ⓜ | Ⓕ |
| (B) | 5–6<br>7–8 | Turn left hands<br>Balance across | ② | ② |
| (C) | 9–10<br>11–12<br>13–16 | Turn left hands<br>Balance across<br>Swing | ③ | ③ |
| (D) | 17–24 | Down the middle and back | ④ | ④ |
| (E) | 25–32 | Poussette | | |

### (A)   Turn right hands, balance across

First couple turn one half turn (two Pas de Basque), holding right hands in a policeman's halt grip, and end up between the second couple. The male takes woman No. 2's left hand in his left and the female takes man No. 2's left hand in her left. They balance in line, doing two Pas de Basque.

*4 BARS*

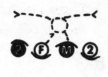

### (B)   Turn left hands, balance across

First couple drop right hands and do a half turn holding left hands with their respective members of the second couple, who join right hands when they meet in the middle (2 bars). They then balance in line, doing two Pas de Basque.

*4 BARS*

### (C)   Turn left hands, balance across, swing

The movement explained in (B) is repeated with the first couple ending up in the middle. Again they balance in line, doing two Pas de Basque. The first couple then swing, cross-wrists.

*8 BARS*

100

## (D) Down the middle and back

The man leads the woman down the middle, between the two lines, and then back up again.

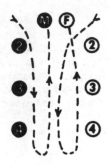

*8 BARS*

## (E) Poussette

Couples Nos. 1 and 2 change places by poussetting round each other.

*8 BARS*

The couple are now ready to restart the routine with the next couple.

# *The Glasgow Highlanders (Strathspey)*

## Basic movements

| | | | |
|---|---|---|---|
| (A) | **Bars 1–8** | Square chain | |
| (B) | 9–12 | Second man leads down | |
| | 13–16 | First man leads up | |
| (C) | 17–24 | Set to partners for eight | |
| (D) | 24–32 | Figure of eight for four | |

Ⓜ　　　　　Ⓕ

②　　　　　②

③　　　　　③

④　　　　　④

As in the previous reel, Scottish Reform, the Glasgow Highlanders is danced in a set, but only two couples take part in the routine, unlike in most reels where there is one major couple and two supporting ones for each routine. The music is a Strathspey and the steps should therefore be Strathspey travelling and setting steps.

On the second chord, as the music starts, the first two couples position themselves as for the Foursome Reel.

### (A) Square chain

The top two couples move round in a square, giving right hands to the other person's partner and left to their own until they come back to their original positions.

*8 BARS*

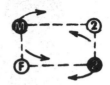

### (B) Second man leads down, first man leads up

As the second man finishes his chain, he takes his partner's right hand in his left hand, and the first woman's left hand in his right hand, and leads them down the set. The male follows.

*4 BARS*

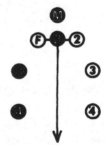

They all three turn at the bottom, and the second man offers both women to the male, who leads them up the set again; the second man follows.

*4 BARS*

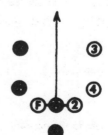

103

### (C)  Set to partners for eight

The women go to their starting positions, and the men stand back to back in the middle. All set for eight bars.

*8 BARS*

### (D)  Figure of eight for four

The top two couples do a figure of eight for four as in the Foursome Reel.

*8 BARS*

On the last bar of the figure of eight, the third man crosses over and stands on the left of his partner. The first man will then lead his partner down the set to stand opposite couple No. 3 so that couples Nos. 3 and 1 are ready to start again. Man No. 2 may now return to his side of the set and face his own partner.

# *Doubles*

As has been pointed out the leading couple in the Glasgow Highlanders and in Scottish Reform only use one other couple to perform their routine. Nearly all the other country dances can be danced in this way by the couple immediately below doubling up and dancing the part of both supporting couples.

This is a very useful fact for the energetic couple who would otherwise find themselves standing uninvolved for two turns at the top of the set before they start, and at the bottom of the set after they have finished.

As in the diagram opposite, couples Nos. 2 and 3 would normally stand idle while the top couple danced with couples Nos. 4 and 5. However, if couple No. 3 is prepared to double up and dance the part of two couples, couple No. 2 may then start. But they must remember to move to the top afterwards, from where they can start again next time for their correct turn.

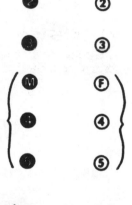

In the second diagram, couple No. 1 would normally move to the bottom of the set but they can dance 'doubles' with couple No. 5 and so keep dancing for longer.

There are some dances for which it is almost impossible to do 'doubles'. These include Hamilton House and The Duke and Duchess of Edinburgh. In this case it is normal to do 'doubles Duke of Perth' instead, and the unwary couple should look out for this. Another alternative which is growing in popularity as the reel itself is becoming more fashionable is 'doubles Reel of the 51st'.

105

# *Mairi's Wedding*

## Basic movements

| | | |
|---|---|---|
| (A) | **Bars 1–4** | Swing partner |
| | **5–6** | Round behind |
| | **7–8** | Left hands |
| (B) | **9–12** | Half figure of eight with first corners |
| | **13–16** | Half figure of eight with second corners |
| (C) | **17–20** | Half figure of eight with first corners |
| | **21–24** | Half figure of eight with second corners |
| (D) | **25–32** | Figures of eight with second and third couples |
| (E) | **33–40** | Circle |

106

## (A) *Swing partner, round behind, left hands*

As in The Duke of Perth, the first couple swing, crossed wrists or crossed forearms, twice round. Then they cast off one, behind their own side, and swing left hands once round.

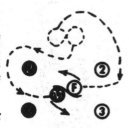

*8 BARS*

## (B) *Half figure of eight with first corners*

As the couple complete their left-handed swing they go straight into a figure of eight with their first corners. The female goes towards man No. 2 passing his right shoulder while the male passes woman No. 3's right shoulder.

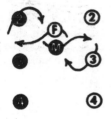

*4 BARS*

## *Half figure of eight with second corners*

When the couple have completed half the figure of eight (i.e., when Ⓕ has passed ⚫ and Ⓜ passed ②), the couple move straight into a figure of eight with second corners. Female passes man No. 3 right shoulders, male passing woman No. 2 right shoulders. As the first couple move into their next figure of eight, the first corners complete their half figure of eight and remain in those positions.

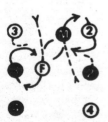

*4 BARS*

### (C) Half figure of eight with first corners

Again half way through the figure of eight the first couple break off and go into a figure of eight with their first corners passing right shoulders. The first corners are now standing the other way round. The female throughout this dance starts her figure of eight by heading towards the man, the male by heading towards the woman.

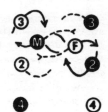

*4 BARS*

### Half figure of eight with second corners

The first couple break out of their figure of eight with first corners and complete the other half of the figure of eight they were enacting with the second corners. Everyone ends up in their original positions except for the first couple.

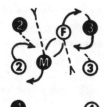

*4 BARS*

### (D) Figure of eight with second and third couples

As they complete this final diagonal figure of eight, the female moves straight into a figure of eight for three with the second couple passing the man left shoulders; while the male does a figure of eight for three with the third couple passing the woman left shoulders.

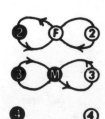

*8 BARS*

### (E) Circle

Finally the male ends up on his own side between the two men and the female ends up similarly between the two women. All then complete a circle; four bars to the right and four bars back again.

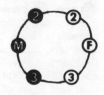

*8 BARS*

108

*Note*

The movements in sections (A) and (B) are complicated and may need further explanation. The top couple start a figure of eight for four with their first corners. When the first corners have changed places, they move straight into a figure of eight for four with their second corners, who also change places. The first couple then complete the figure of eight for four with their first corners so that they change back to their original positions. Similarly, they complete the figure of eight for four with their second corners allowing them to move back to their original positions.

To clarify further, I have traced out below the path which the male and the female follow when completing their four half figure of eights in sections (A) and (B).

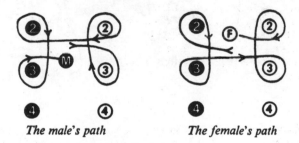

*The male's path*          *The female's path*

It must be remembered that couples Nos. 2 and 3 will not be standing in one place, as implied above, but will be moving diagonally across the set

# *Petronella*

THIS DANCE was introduced by one Nathanial Gow at his annual ball in Edinburgh, in 1820. It is described in *The Ballroom* which was published in 1827.

## Basic movements

(A) **Bars 1–4** Twirl into the middle
          5–8 Twirl into partner's place

(B)       9–12 Twirl into middle
      13–16 Twirl into own place

(C)    17–24 Down the middle and back

(D)    25–32 Poussette

Ⓜ      Ⓕ

❷      ②

❸      ③

❹      ④

### (A)  Twirl into the middle, twirl into partner's place

The female, leading off on her right foot, twirls a complete turn in two Pas de Basque and ends up at the top of the set, in the middle facing her partner.

He, similarly, has twirled (two Pas de Basque) into position between couple No. 3. Both then do two Pas de Basque on the spot facing each other.

*4 BARS*

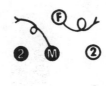

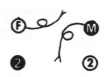

They then twirl into their partners' original place and do two Pas de Basque on the spot.

*4 BARS*

### (B)  Twirl into middle, twirl into own place

Again they twirl (two Pas de Basque), the male now standing at the top of the set looking down the middle and the female standing opposite. Both then do two Pas de Basque on the spot.

*4 BARS*

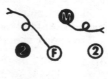

111

Finally, they twirl back into their original positions, doing two more Pas de Basque on the spot once they arrive there. It is important to note that the top couple have not so far touched each other.

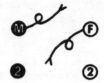

*4 BARS*

### (C)  *Down the middle and back*

The male now takes the female's right hand and leads her down the middle between the two lines of the set and back up again.

*8 BARS*

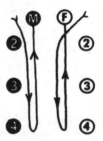

### (D)  *Poussette*

The top couple and couple No. 2 now 'poussette' round each other, changing places. The couple is now ready to start again.

*8 BARS*

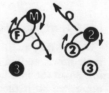

As can be seen, couple No. 2 take very little part in the routine. They can join in more by twirling into the spaces which the first couple vacate in sections (A) and (B), as opposite. They can then follow the first couple down the middle of the set. But at the bottom they must stop and raise their arms, so letting the top couple pass between them. This is so that the top couple arrive at the top of the set above the second couple, providing reason for the poussette which enables them to change places.

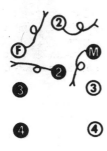

# The Dashing White Sergeant

## Basic movements

| | | | | Wing | Centre | Wing |
|---|---|---|---|---|---|---|
| (A) | **Bars 1–8** | Circle | | | | |
| (B) | 9–12 | Set and turn | | ②——①——② | | |
| | 13–16 | Set and turn | | | | |
| (C) | 17–24 | Figure of eight | | | | |
| (D) | 25–28 | Forward and back | | ④——❸——④ | | |
| (E) | 29–32 | Forward and through | | Wing | Centre | Wing |

THIS REEL is danced in lines of three. A line must contain one man and two women or one woman and two men. The routine is enacted by two lines facing each other.

### (A) Circle

All six dancers join hands and circle four Pas de Basque to the left and four Pas de Basque back again.

*8 BARS*

## (B)  Set and turn, set and turn

The centre man or woman (No. 1 or No. 3) sets to and turns one of his or her 'wings' . . .

*4 BARS*

. . . then sets to and turns the other.

*4 BARS*

## (C)  Figure of eight

Then the centres do a figure of eight with their two 'wings'.

*8 BARS*

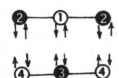

## (D)  Forward and back

The two lines join hands, advance towards each other, stamping their feet at the point of closest proximity, and then retreat. It is not considered polite to stamp on the toes of the person facing one.

*4 BARS*

## (E)  Forward and through

Both lines advance again, this time breaking through by one line raising their arms so that the other line can pass underneath. The lines then meet other lines and repeat the same routine. It is interesting to note that in the past this reel was never danced so that lines of a woman and two men, or lines of a man and two women could meet. However, today this happens regularly.

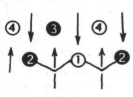

*8 BARS*
115

# Index of Symbols

The male or man No. 1.     Ⓜ

The female or woman No. 1.     Ⓕ

Man No. 2 and woman No. 3 or first corners.     ② ③

Woman No. 2 and man No. 3 or second corners.     ③ ②

Couple No. 3 'setting'.     ③ ③

Female and man No. 2 'turning'—two hands.     Ⓕ②

Couple No. 2 'swinging' clockwise, crossed wrists or crossed forearms.

Couple No. 2 'swinging' clockwise—right arms linked.

Couple No. 3 'swinging' anti-clockwise—left arms linked.

Man and woman No. 2 'swinging'—reversed arms linked.

Couple No. 1 'turning'—policeman's halt grip.

Figure of eight with three.

Figure of eight with four.

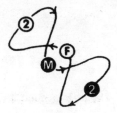

Weaving figure of eight.

First three couples doing a circle.

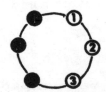

Casting off—couple No. 1 casts off one place.

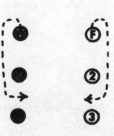

Teapot of three—right hands, clockwise.

Teapot of four—left hands, anti-clockwise.

Holding hands in line.

Balancing in line.

Poussette—couple No. 1 poussetting into couple No. 2's position and vice versa.

Square chain with top two couples.

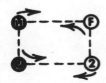

119